To Emily & George
C. B.

To my father
L. G.

Text copyright © 2017 by Chris Butterworth
Illustrations copyright © 2017 by Lucia Gaggiotti

First U.S. edition 2018

Library of Congress Catalog Card Number pending
ISBN 978-0-7636-9594-1

18 19 20 21 22 CCP 10 9 8 7 6 5 4 3 2

Printed in Shenzhen, Guangdong, China

This book was typeset in VAG Rounded.
The illustrations were done in mixed media.

Candlewick Press
99 Dover Street
Somerville, Massachusetts 02144

visit us at www.candlewick.com

Chris Butterworth

How Does My Home Work?

illustrated by Lucia Gaggiotti

CANDLEWICK PRESS

YOU do neat things every day in your home.

Flip the switch, and the light goes on.

Push a button, and the TV comes on.

Turn on the faucet, and clean water comes out.

Take a drink from the refrigerator, and it's cool and fresh.

These things seem like magic—but they're not.
So how do they happen?

Under the floors and behind the walls of your home are pipes that bring in water and natural gas and wires that bring in electricity, day and night.

clean, cold water IN
clean, hot water IN
dirty water OUT
electricity IN
natural gas IN

Circuit breaker

Gas meter

Water tank

This means you can turn on the lights and the faucets, watch TV, and keep your food cool in the refrigerator.

All the machines that people use every day need energy to make them work.

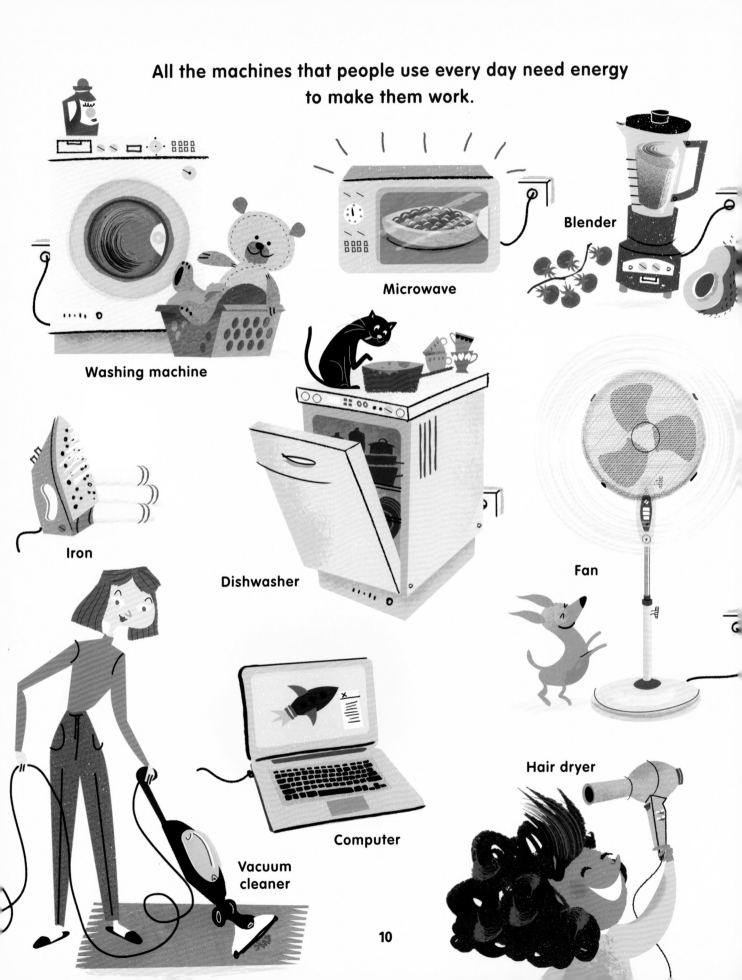

Washing machine

Microwave

Blender

Iron

Dishwasher

Fan

Vacuum cleaner

Computer

Hair dryer

Kettle

Toaster

Light

Mixer

TV and
game console

Space heater

Refrigerator

Lamp

Radio

Mobile phone

11

WHERE DOES **ELECTRiCiTY** COME FROM?

Electricity occurs naturally in the form of lightning. The energy from just one bolt of lightning could boil enough water for more than fifty thousand cups of hot chocolate! But of course we can't use lightning to power our homes: the electricity we use is made in power stations.

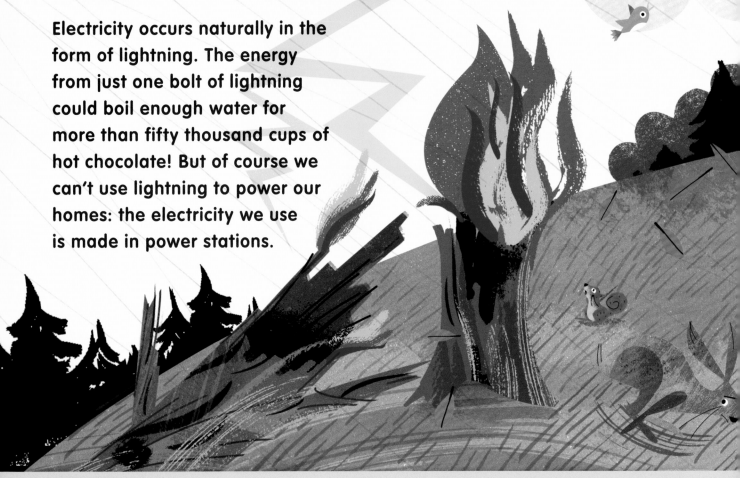

Most power stations burn natural gas or coal to heat water, but this sends smoke containing harmful chemicals into the air.

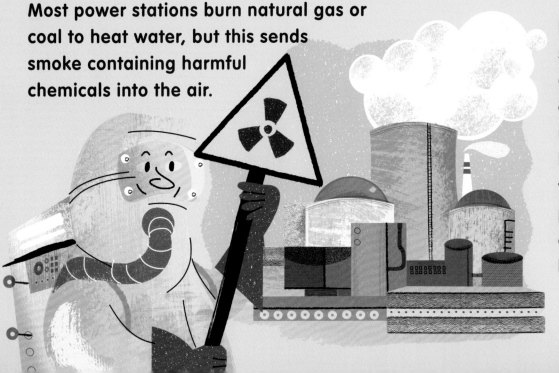

Nuclear power stations most often use an element called uranium to heat water. The waste from this process can be dangerous if not handled properly.

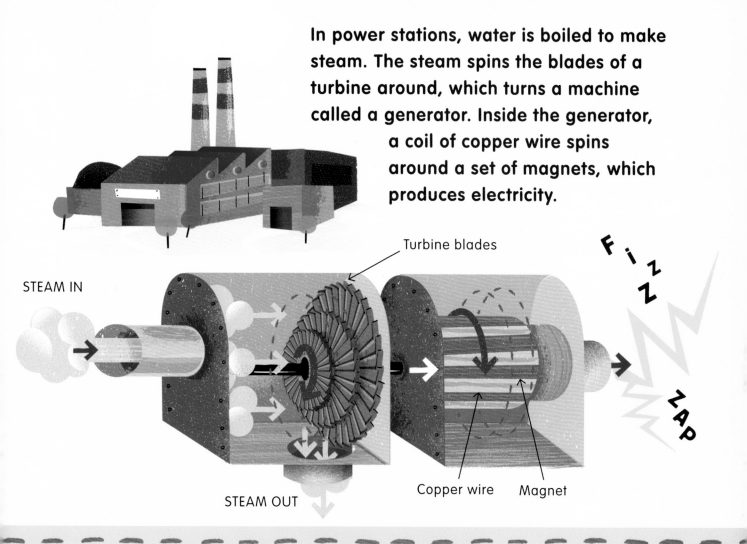

In power stations, water is boiled to make steam. The steam spins the blades of a turbine around, which turns a machine called a generator. Inside the generator, a coil of copper wire spins around a set of magnets, which produces electricity.

Turbine blades

STEAM IN

FIZZ

ZAP

STEAM OUT

Copper wire

Magnet

There are cleaner ways to make electricity. . . .

The power of fast-moving water can be used to turn turbines.

Wind turbines make electricity using wind power.

Solar panels absorb sunlight, which can be used to produce electricity.

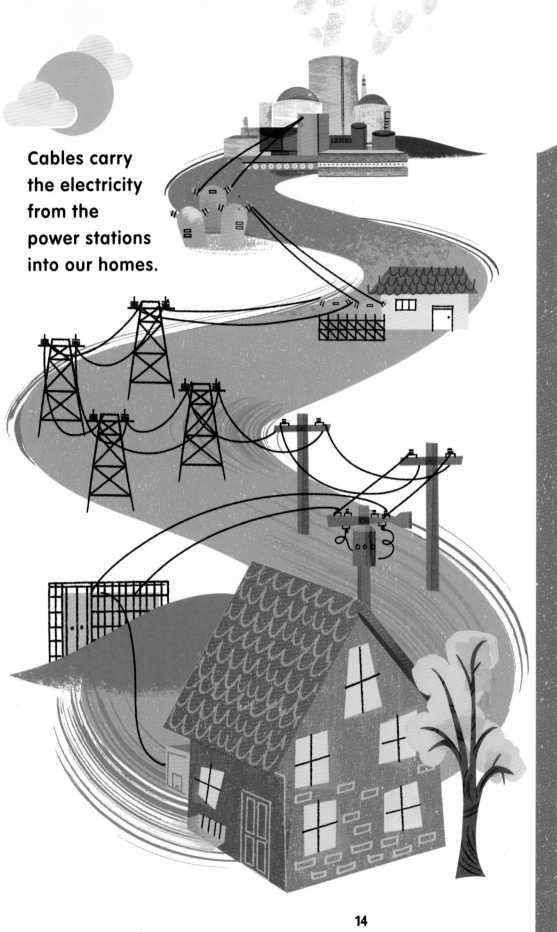

Cables carry the electricity from the power stations into our homes.

One wire takes electricity to the switch.

Light switch

If the sun has gone down and you're still busy, you can turn a light on.

Another wire goes from the switch to the light.

When you flip the switch ON, a piece of metal creates a connection between the two wires that allows electricity to pass from one wire to the next.

Electricity flows to the lightbulb, and it begins to glow! When you flip the switch OFF, you break the connection and the light goes out.

WHERE DOES WATER

Along with electricity, homes need clean water. Water is always moving and changing: it can exist as a gas like in the clouds; a solid, such as snow on mountain peaks; or a liquid, such as falling rain or in rivers and streams. The water we use in our homes is often from big lakes called reservoirs.

1. At the water treatment plant, the reservoir water is strained to get rid of the big things floating in it, such as sticks and leaves.

2. The strained water is left to stand in large tanks. More dirt sinks, making a layer of sludge at the bottom.

Sludge

COME FROM?

Reservoir water can be full of dirt, so it needs cleaning before it is safe to drink.

Rainwater soaks back into the earth and can collect in wells underground. We use pumps to bring the water to the surface.

Water treatment plant

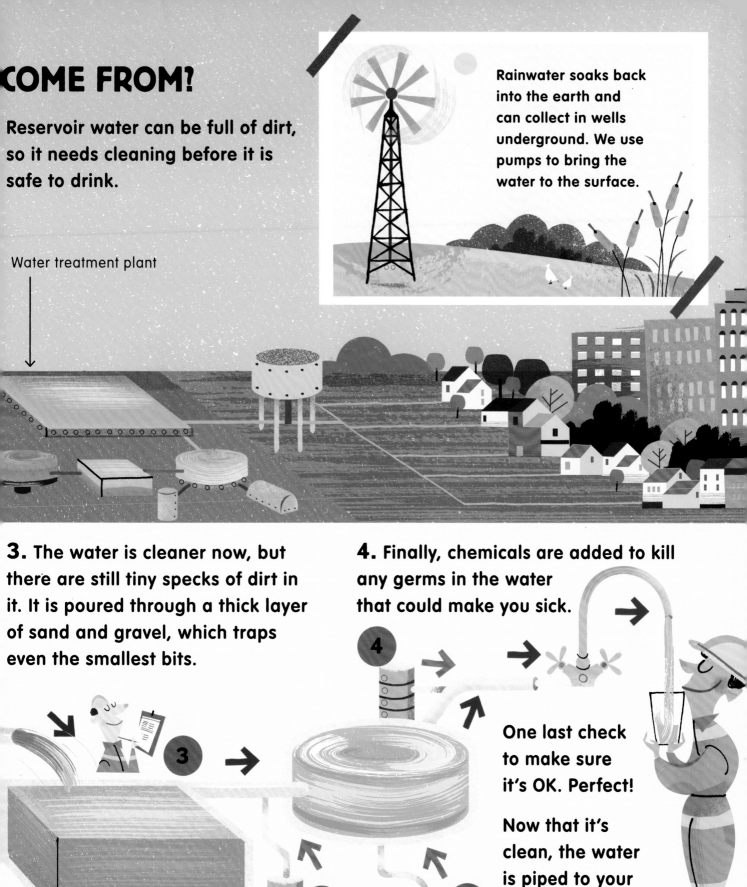

3. The water is cleaner now, but there are still tiny specks of dirt in it. It is poured through a thick layer of sand and gravel, which traps even the smallest bits.

4. Finally, chemicals are added to kill any germs in the water that could make you sick.

One last check to make sure it's OK. Perfect!

Now that it's clean, the water is piped to your home.

Sand and Gravel

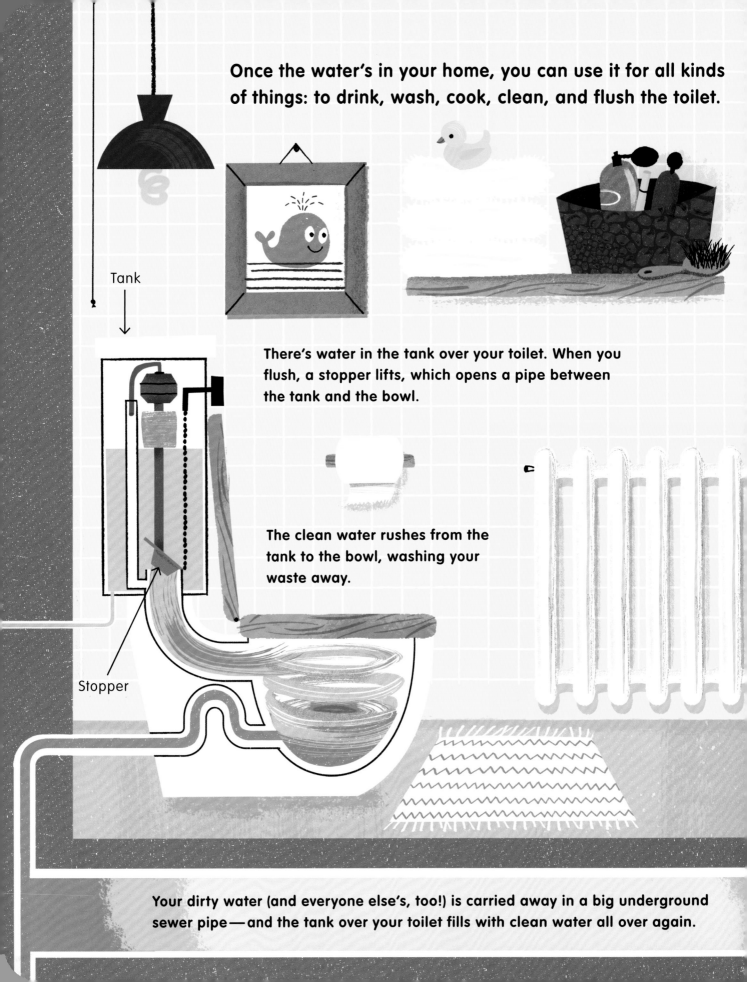

Once the water's in your home, you can use it for all kinds of things: to drink, wash, cook, clean, and flush the toilet.

Tank

There's water in the tank over your toilet. When you flush, a stopper lifts, which opens a pipe between the tank and the bowl.

The clean water rushes from the tank to the bowl, washing your waste away.

Stopper

Your dirty water (and everyone else's, too!) is carried away in a big underground sewer pipe—and the tank over your toilet fills with clean water all over again.

Time to wash your hands!

When the faucet is OFF, the pipe is blocked by a stopper so that the water can't get out.

Closed →

When you turn the faucet ON, you lift the stopper. The pipe is unblocked, and the clean water flows into the basin.

Open →

After you've used water in your home, it goes back to the rivers and the sea—
but because it's dirty, it has to be cleaned very carefully first.

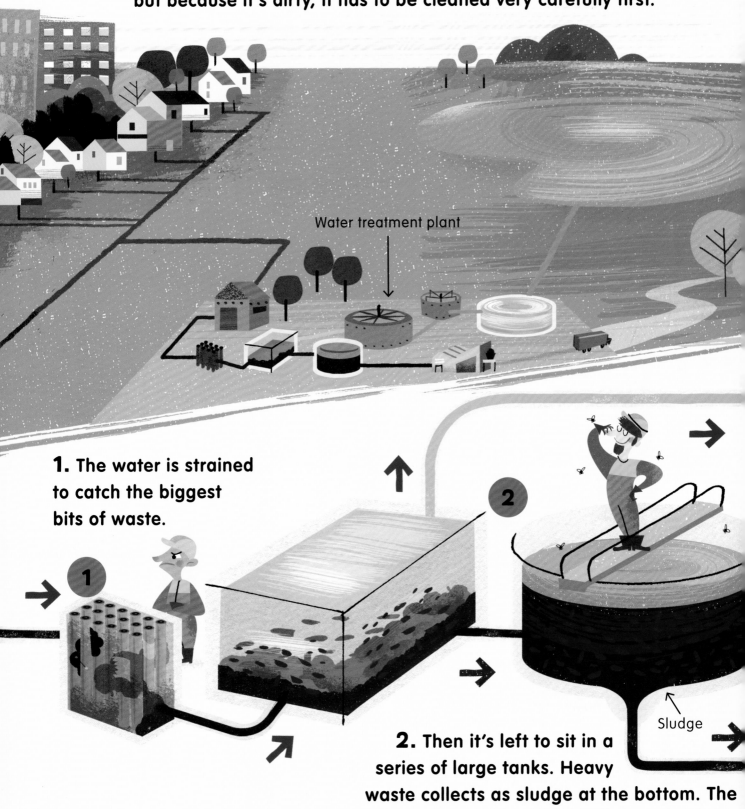

Water treatment plant

1. The water is strained to catch the biggest bits of waste.

Sludge

2. Then it's left to sit in a series of large tanks. Heavy waste collects as sludge at the bottom. The water goes to another tank for more cleaning.

3. In this tank, a large fan shoots air bubbles through the water. This helps the good germs to eat up the bad germs that make you sick.

4. The water is nearly clean! Chemicals are added to kill any leftover germs.

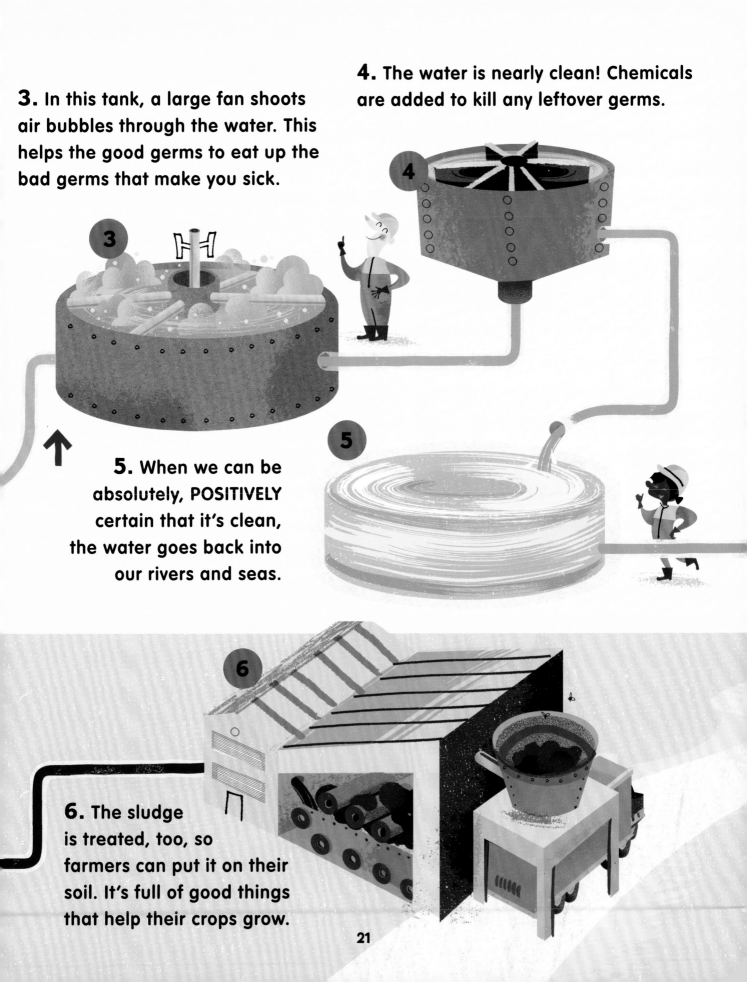

5. When we can be absolutely, POSITIVELY certain that it's clean, the water goes back into our rivers and seas.

6. The sludge is treated, too, so farmers can put it on their soil. It's full of good things that help their crops grow.

WHERE DOES **NATURAL GAS** COME FROM?

Now you know where electricity and clean water come from!
Many homes also use natural gas for heat and cooking.

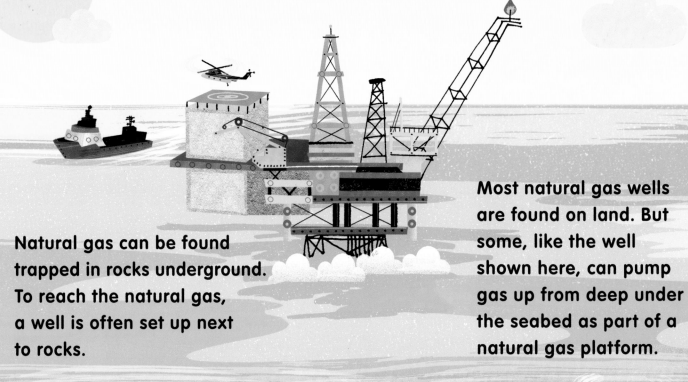

Natural gas can be found
trapped in rocks underground.
To reach the natural gas,
a well is often set up next
to rocks.

Most natural gas wells
are found on land. But
some, like the well
shown here, can pump
gas up from deep under
the seabed as part of a
natural gas platform.

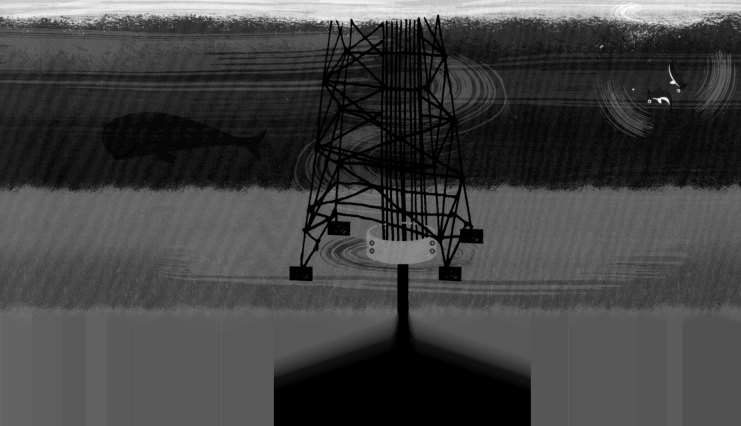

Natural gas contains chemicals that need to be removed. It has to be piped to a factory to separate out the natural gas you will use in your home.

Processing factory

Then it can be stored in giant underground tanks.

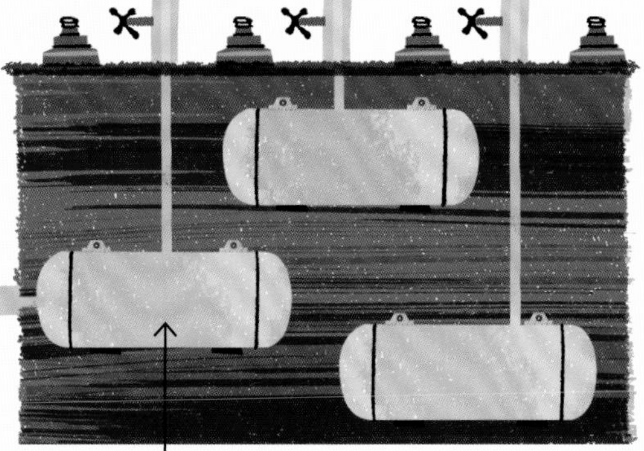

Cleaned gas storage

The natural gas is piped straight to your home.

Now you know more about how your home works!
We use lots of energy to give us electricity, heat,
and clean water whenever we want.

SAVING ENERGY

Energy is precious—let's not waste it!

HOW MANY OF THESE THINGS CAN YOU DO!

TURN OFF LIGHTS WHEN YOU LEAVE A ROOM.

TURN OFF THE FAUCET WHILE BRUSHING YOUR TEETH.

TURN TVs AND COMPUTERS OFF AT NIGHT INSTEAD OF LEAVING THEM ON STANDBY.

TAKE SHORT SHOWERS.

REMEMBER TO CLOSE THE REFRIGERATOR DOOR.

RECYCLE AS MUCH AS YOU CAN.

WHEN COOKING, ONLY BOIL AS MUCH WATER AS YOU NEED.

PUT ON EXTRA CLOTHES WHEN YOU'RE COLD INSTEAD OF TURNING UP THE HEAT.

COLLECT RAINWATER TO WATER YOUR PLANTS.

AUTHOR'S NOTE

It's easy to take home comforts for granted—the clean water and energy that help make our homes safe and healthy. I hope knowing more about how a home works will help us all care more about where our heat, electricity, and water come from and how we use them.

iLLUSTRATOR'S NOTE

My father was an interior designer, and when I was little I used to copy his drawings of rooms, apartments, or whole houses. This book reminded me of those days, which are so dear to me. But I didn't know what went on behind the scenes until now. I hope it will be really informative for children . . . and for adults!

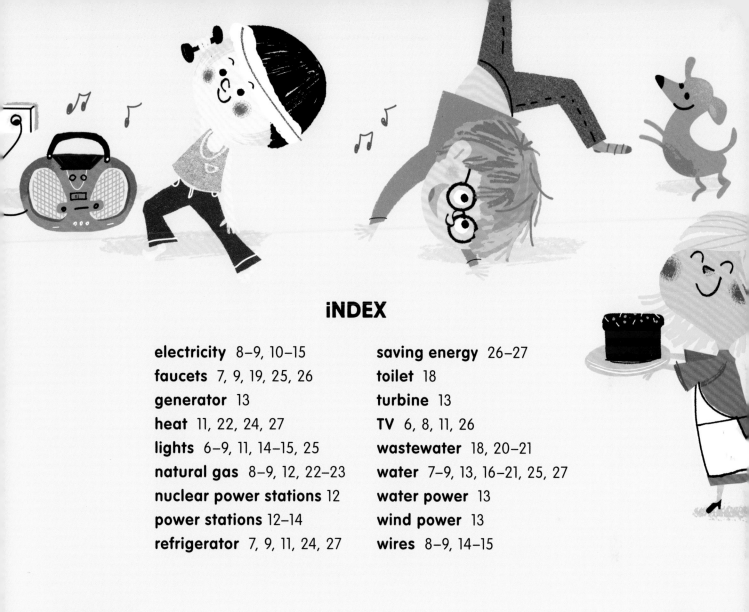

iNDEX

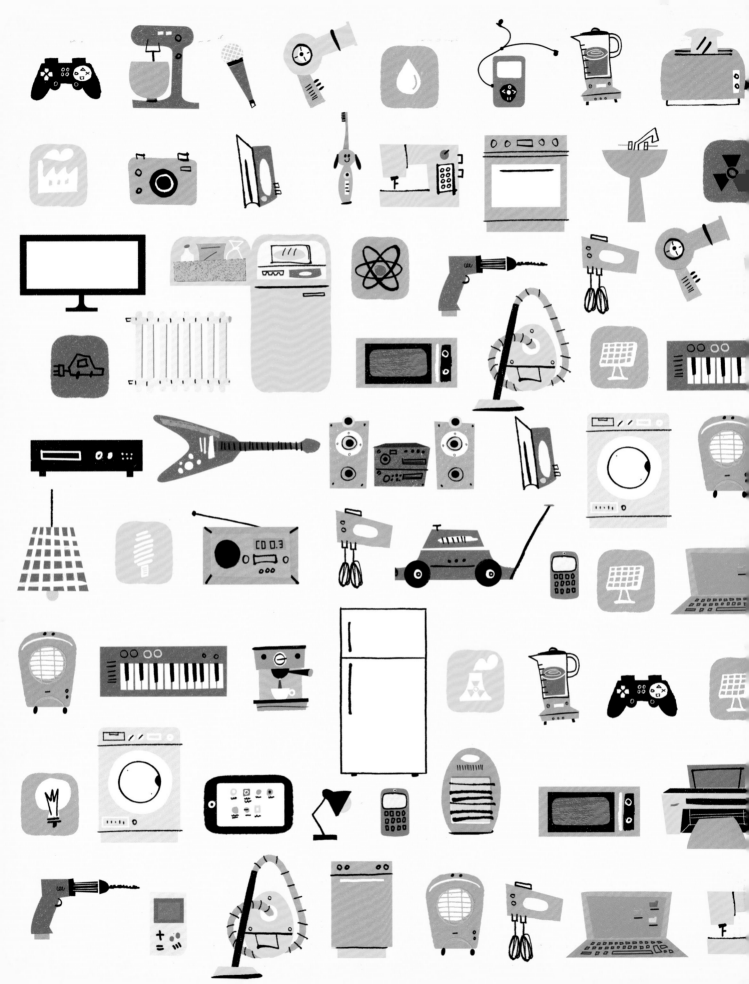